W.C.N Randolph

Reply of the Rector and Visitors of the University of VA.

W.C.N Randolph

Reply of the Rector and Visitors of the University of VA.

ISBN/EAN: 9783337035914

Printed in Europe, USA, Canada, Australia, Japan

Cover: Foto ©ninafisch / pixelio.de

More available books at **www.hansebooks.com**

REPLY

RECTOR AND VISITORS

UNIVERSITY OF VA,

REMONSTRANCE ON RECENT CHANGES IN THE REQUIREMENTS

DEGREE OF MASTER OF ARTS.

UNIVERSITY OF VIRGINIA,
Charlottesville, Va.
1892.

Extracts from the Minutes of the Proceedings of the Rector and Visitors.

"The Committee on the Conduct of Schools recommends the establishment of a general Academical degree to be known as the Bachelor of Arts degree, which all Academical students shall be required to take before proceeding to the higher degree of Master of Arts. The course of instruction for this B. A. degree shall be essentially different in scope from that provided for the M. A. degree; which latter shall be given to such Academical students only as shall have given satisfactory evidence of having mastered some special line of study after taking the general or B. A. degree." (MINUTES, 11 July, 1888.)

"The scope and purpose of instruction given in the subjects required for the B. A. degree shall have for chief end a sound general knowledge of each subject. The old nomenclature of Proficient shall be dropped in regard to the rating of candidates, who pass successfully the B. A. examinations in the subjects required." (MINUTES, 9 Feb., 1889.)

"The requirements for the B. A. degree shall consist of graduation in the B. A. courses in Latin, Greek or Logic, Pure Mathematics or General Astronomy, French or Spanish or Italian, German or English, General History, and two of the four sciences (Chemistry, Physics, Biology, and Geology). The examinations shall in all cases be in writing and the standard shall be rigidly three-fourths." (MINUTES, 28 June, 1890.)

"In order to attain the M. A. degree it shall be necessary for every applicant to have first taken the B. A. degree. After taking that degree he shall take an advanced course of University instruction in some four Schools embracing for example—

i. Latin, Greek, Moral Philosophy, one Teutonic and one Romance Language;

ii. Mathematics, Natural Philosophy, Applied Chemistry, Mineralogy and Geology;

iii. Latin, Greek, Mathematics, one Teutonic and one Romance Language;

or any combination of four Schools in the Academical Department, which in the judgment of the Faculty shall be the full equivalent of any of the above groups." (MINUTES, 29 June, 1891.)

WM. H. PROUT,
BOOK AND JOB PRINTER,
CHARLOTTESVILLE, VA.

REMONSTRANCE

ON

Recent Changes in the Degree of Master of Arts

AT THE

UNIVERSITY OF VIRGINIA.

———

To the Rector and Board of Visitors of the University of Virginia :

We, the undersigned, Masters of Arts of the University and Students pursuing the course hitherto marked out for the attainment of that degree, respectfully request the Board to reconsider their action in changing the requisites for the degree of Master of Arts of the University of Virginia. At the meeting of the Board in June, 1891, the following resolution was passed: "That in order to attain the M. A. degree it shall be necessary for every applicant to have first taken the B. A. degree; after taking that degree, he shall take an advanced course of University instruction in some four of the schools. These four schools shall embrace—

I.   1. LATIN.
    2. GREEK.
    3. ONE TEUTONIC AND ONE ROMANCE LANGUAGE.
    4. MORAL PHILOSOPHY, OR HISTORY; or,

II.   1. MATHEMATICS.
    2. NATURAL PHILOSOPHY.
    3. APPLIED CHEMISTRY.

    4. NATURAL HISTORY AND BIOLOGY, OR MINER-
       ALOGY AND GEOLOGY; or,

III. 1. LATIN.

    2. GREEK.

    3. MORAL PHILOSOPHY, OR ONE TEUTONIC AND
       ONE ROMANCE LANGUAGE.

    4. MATHEMATICS, OR NATURAL PHILOSOPHY, OR
       MATHEMATICS AND ASTRONOMY; or,

IV. The Faculty may, in their judgment, in lieu of any
of these four schools make a combination of any four
schools in the Academic Department, which shall be the
full equivalent of any of the groups named above."

We consider that the degree of Master of Arts of the
University of Virginia is the highest degree conferred in
the United States on undergraduate students. Such it is
acknowledged to be by all who are competent to form an
opinion entitled to value.

Prof. J. H. Wright, of Harvard, in an article in the *Lon-
don Classical Review* for February 2, 1890, says: "As a
rule the Master of Arts in the United States means little
except that its holder has at some time received a B. A.
degree. At the better colleges the candidate is required to
show that he paid some attention to liberal studies for a
year or two after receiving his B. A. degree. At the University of Virginia, however, this degree has a singularly
honorable position; the conditions on which it is bestowed
are severe, and it stands for distinct and high attainments
in scholarship."

We submit that the peculiar distinction universally accorded to this degree, as it now exists, is of inestimable
value to the University, that its reputation is worth preserving, that a radical change in the *nature* of its requirements will ruin its present "honorable position" and

necessitate the acquisition of a new reputation, that any change approximating our degree to those of other institutions in America will destroy its individuality and impair its usefulness.

The Master of Arts degree has for sixty years been the distinctive feature of this institution, and the University guarantees the scholarship of all who bear it; as long as it is given, the fame of the University must largely depend on the acquirements of its Masters. A host of men have left these walls bearing this honorable title who justly regard it as the outward indication of high attainments in the fields of literature and science, and therefore bear it with pride. Most of these have justified the high hopes entertained of them by their *Alma Mater*—they have alike reflected credit on themselves and on her.

The great renown in which our M. A. is held, both at home and abroad, rests upon two pillars: the immense field over which it extends and the high standard of attainment necessary for success in each department of knowledge. Take away either of these supports, and the other alone is not sufficient to hold us up; the first bears the fame of our degree for a liberal education, the last carries our reputation for high attainment in all the departments of such an education. Without the one, the M. A. becomes merely a special degree, showing perhaps high development on one or two lines, but is no longer the synonym for a well rounded and polished gentleman—without the other, our degree men are *dilettantes*,* possessed of that most baneful of all acquirements—a little learning.

The field now covered by this degree is a large one, comprising graduation at a high standard in Latin, Mathematics, Moral Philosophy, Natural Philosophy, Chemistry, French, German, and Greek. Who can say that a

*Dilettanti.

deep insight into all of these is not essential to a liberal education? Who would say that more is required?

The Master of Arts degree provided for by the action of the Board is either a post-graduate degree or an undergraduate degree of lower standard than the old one; the Bachelor's degree is made a prerequisite, and the Master's degree may then be attained by graduation in any four schools approved by the Faculty; if it be meant by this requirement that no one can get an M. A. unless he has graduated in four schools after getting a B. A., the character of man who will in future apply for our distinctive degree will be changed; there are few undergraduate students so well* prepared that they cannot profitably devote their time to the Senior classes of the various schools; to such students the B. A. opens no new course of study, but merely a review of his high-school work. As a manifest consequence of this fact, this alternative presents itself: either the high-school graduate will seek other fields of study, and the degree will be neglected, or since the amount of preparation for the B. A. course is much less, students of poor attainments and very young years will present themselves, and instead of men of eighteen or twenty entering the University, lads of fifteen or sixteen, who may prefer to get their Academic training at this place instead of at school, will come in; and since the entire freedom from restraint, which is granted to the men here, could not in justice be allowed to those who would be but boys in years, our whole system must necessarily be changed and the surveillance and restraint of high school and college be introduced.

If the language of the Board be interpreted to mean that any man who has graduated in four schools and obtained proficiency in a sufficient number of classes to entitle him to the degree of Bachelor of Arts will receive his

*Doubtless "ill" is meant.

M. A., we submit that the standard of the University's distinctive degree, and therefore the standard of the University, has been lowered; for the present requirements. there would be substituted a requirement of four proficiencies and four graduations. This provision that the Schools elected are to be approved by the Faculty must be a dead letter, since the discretion given to them is an arbitrary discretion, without any rule to guide them, and therefore they could not fairly exercise it against a B. A. who had graduated in four Schools. According to this interpretation a well-prepared man could with ease accomplish the work required for the M. A. degree in two years, whereas at Harvard it was only after long and mature consideration that the B. A. course was shortened from four to three years.

According to either interpretation a man might be an M. A. of the University of Virginia without having more than a slight knowledge of Latin; he might be an M. A. without having even heard that there is such a thing as Calculus, or without knowing a principle of Psychology or a law of Logic. He might receive his degree without having shown any greater knowledge of foreign languages than just enough to enable him to pass his examinations in the intermediate classes in Latin and French; he might be wholly ignorant of Chemistry or of Physics. Is it becoming the dignity of the University to confer its highest degree upon one who has shown no scholarly knowledge of the languages, ancient or modern, and who may not have stood a single examination on Pure Mathematics? It would seem a misnomer to confer the degree of *Master of Arts* on one who may have confined himself entirely in his senior studies to Science or to Literature, and who has passed through his lower studies under a depreciated standard. He is a master in only half of the field; hitherto the title has been conferred only on those who had graduated in the highest classes in each of the prescribed schools; it is neither right nor just for the University to mislead the public by conferring its time-honored degree on men of inferior attainments.

The B. A. course, as it now stands, embraces merely those branches of study commonly taught at our high schools and colleges, and any well-prepared man, coming from any of those colleges or schools, would find at his first entrance into the University but little difficulty in passing the examinations on those subjects which he was taught while at school.

In the proposed scheme of the new M. A. it is possible to become a Master of Arts of the University of Virginia with absolutely no knowledge of Greek and with such knowledge of Latin only as is required to pass the examinations in the intermediate class in that school, which, as stated above, is simply the work now required of those high-school pupils prepared to enter the senior class. The proposed change is a blow to the study of Greek, which must certainly result in serious consequences. We are fully aware that it is now a popular tendency to regulate Greek to the limbo of the lost arts and to substitute Science in its place. While we fully appreciate the vital importance of scientific study, we would enter a respectful protest against the University lending a helping hand to what foreshadows the death of the study of Greek at the University. A large percentage of those who take the senior class in Greek are at present those who have as their ultimate goal the Master's degree, and if an avowedly easier road is opened to them many will desert the field of Greek altogether.

It is doubtless contended that the standard will not be lowered by the threatened change because the professors will advance what are now their intermediate classes to the position which the senior classes occupy, and they in turn will be made more difficult. We apprehend that even supposing to be true it would be very undesirable, for there can be no possible complaint from any quarter that our senior classes are too easy; they cover completely the ground they were intended to cover; it must be remembered that most academic students come to the University not in order to learn everything that is to be known on a subject, not to pursue it in all its ramifications, but only to get a knowledge of the fundamental laws and principles that govern it, such as becomes an educated man to know. The *Specialists* must always be in the minority; so their name implies. Any material increase in the difficulty of our senior classes must place them in the rank of post-graduate and special studies, and to that extent we close the door to the majority of students.

But this result we do not dread so much as that other and we fear more probable consequence, to-wit: that in the effort to popularize and populate their classes the professors will bend from that high and rigid standard which has made our University world-renowned. A student who has the choice of many departments for his degree will inevitably take those which can be attained with least difficulty; a large falling off will follow in those schools which are intrinsically more difficult, though, for that very reason, perhaps, more useful, and the professor must stand by and see his school decimated, or must make it more popular at the expense of the requisite labor and its usefulness. It is not hard to conceive which course he will adopt.

We do not wish the Board to understand from this that we are against all change of the M. A. degree. Such is not the case. We agree heartily that some *option* should be allowed, and to that extent that the degree be broadened; that is another and a different question; but, to a man, we stand convinced that any change in the standard, that *summum bonum* of our system, or even the appearance of any such change, should be carefully avoided.

We would also beg to express to the Board our fullest confidence that they take a deep and abiding interest in the welfare of our *Alma Mater*, and that they will always do what appears in their wise judgment to best serve and benefit her.

LIST OF SIGNERS OF THE REMONSTRANCE.

*Masters of Arts.**

(49) CHARLES MARSHALL,
(50) WILLIAM WIRT HENRY,
(51) JAMES PLEASANTS,
 JOHN L. WILLIAMS,
(54) WILLIAM DINWIDDIE,
 GEO. TUCKER HARRISON,
(61) JAMES L. DINWIDDIE.

(82) KENNETH A. BAIN,
 JOHN B. JENKINS,
 G. HARRISON SMITH,
 JAS. H. WOODROW,
(83) GEORGE McK. BAIN,
 LEIGH CARROLL,
 R. GOODWYN RHETT,
 THOMAS FITZHUGH,
(84) WISTER ARCHER,
 COOPER D. SCHMITT,

(86) UPTON W. MUIR,
 JAMES W. S. PETERS,
(87) JAMES N. ANDERSON,
(88) J. H. C. BAGBY,
 WALLACE F. BROWN,
 RO. SPRATT COCKRELL,
 RALEIGH C. MINOR,
(89) WILLIAM DINWIDDIE, Jr.,
 MINTON W. TALBOT,
 FIELDING L. TAYLOR,
 JAMES B. WOODS,
(90) ALBERT B. DINWIDDIE,
 JOSEPH B. DUNN, Jr.,
 HALSTEAD S. HEDGES,
 JAMES B. LOVETT,
 WALTER F. TAYLOR,
(91) THOS. J. RANDOLPH,
 ROBERT F. WILLIAMS, Jr.

Candidates.

MALLORY K. CANNON,
R. E. LEE DINWIDDIE,
R. E. LEE FARMER,
FRANK L. HIMEL,

MURRAY M. McGUIRE,
J. MARKHAM MARSHALL,
EDWARD F. MAYBERRY,
HARRISON RANDOLPH.

*Proportion of signers: Ante-bellum, 7 out of 145; Post-bellum, 28 out of 108.

Reply of the Visitors to the Remonstrance.

To the "M. A. Committee," University of Virginia :

Gentlemen :—Your protest against the changes made by the Board of Visitors in the requirements for the degree of Master of Arts of the University of Virginia, was duly received by the Rector and laid before the Visitors at their last meeting in November, 1891.

This protest was signed by W. F. Taylor, M. A., as "Chairman of the Committee," by thirty-four other Masters of Arts, and by eight young gentlemen, who are now "applicants for the M. A. degree."

The Board of Visitors was unable at that time to give the protest any consideration, as the November meeting was suddenly called to deal with business of a practical and pressing nature, which claimed the whole attention of the Rector and Visitors up to the hour of adjournment.

This will account for the delay in replying to the protest, which has since that time had the most respectful and careful consideration of the Visitors.

The paper seems to the Visitors to have been hastily written under a misapprehension as to the real character and scope of the changes made in the requirements for both the M. A. and B. A. degrees.

As the Visitors believe that these changes, if clearly understood, must claim the hearty support of all true friends of the University, they shall not content themselves with a simple refusal to reconsider their action, but most cheerfully lay before your Committee their reasons for having ordered these changes, and for now declining, after maturely weighing your protest, to recede from steps taken after the most cautious deliberation by *a unanimous vote of the Board*.

To the mind of the Visitors, it has long been a source of weakness to the University that there has been here no reputable undergraduate degree, which appealed to any large number of students of fair ability and determined industry, who were desirous, not of the specialistic training of a school-master, but of a sound, general knowledge of such subjects as are commonly deemed essential in any scheme of liberal education. (See "*Report on the Conduct of Schools*," University of Va., February 9th, 1889.)

That the old B. A. was such a degree will scarcely be seriously maintained by any one who knows its history and "traditions." It always carried with it a distinct flavor of academic defeat, and was generally regarded as a sort of "consolation stakes" for those who failed in the race for the overshadowing "*Grand Prize*"—the M. A.

Few men ever cared to apply for it prior to the war, and, though the Faculty, apparently keenly alive to the desirability of such a degree and fully aware of the strength that such a degree would give the University, have time and again sought to frame a B. A. course, at once sound as to scholarship and attractive to the great body of students, the results indicate that there was something inherently wrong in the various schemes proposed and adopted.

Five times in the twenty years from 1865 to 1885 (an average of once in every four years), were the requirements for the B. A. degree changed, yet the fact remained that but few students applied for that degree.

Such was the state of things when the Visitors, in 1888, determined to give their attention to the existing requirements for degrees in the University.

Naturally, they approached with diffidence a subject which apparently had baffled the continued efforts of those who seemed best equipped for dealing with such a problem.

Still, the problem was unsolved, the question seemed a pressing one, and the Visitors could not shirk it consistently with their responsible position as the recognized custodians of the best interests of the University.

They first considered the B. A. degree, and, on conferring with a committee appointed by the Faculty touching the subject, were assured in the most emphatic manner by some of the ablest professors in the University that "the requirements for the B. A. degree, then in force, imperatively demanded revision."

It is needless to say that the Visitors had the highest respect for the tried loyalty and academic experience of the Faculty, and that, in the changes, which they saw to be imperative, they desired to avail themselves at every step of the counsel of these faithful servants of the University. A full and free discussion with the committee of all the points involved, developed, as was to be expected, a wide diversity of views.

Still, two facts seemed to be evident: (1) that there was a sort of stigma attaching to the old B. A. degree here, which had come to be regarded (whether rightly or wrongly) as a sort of public advertisement of academic failure; (2) that there was an imperative need for a reputable B. A. degree, the requirements of which should be so framed as to attract the great body of academic students, and induce them to remain long enough in the University to secure the basis of a liberal education.

It was, indeed, a startling fact to the Board to find, on investigation of the records for years past, that, of all the students in the University, *little more than two-fifths remained more than one year*, and that only *one* student in *eighteen* remained *four* years.

On careful investigation, the inherent faults of the former B. A. schemes seemed two-fold: (1) that the course of instruction did not possess a *character and spirit of its own*, but was simply a fragment of the semi-specialistic training required for the M. A. degree, the requirements for the B. A. degree being satisfied in several schools if the candidate attained in his examinations a certain percentage of marks (lower than required for "graduation") or a smaller volume of *the identical work* demanded of a student, who was seeking the training of a specialist; (2) that, by retaining the old nomenclature of "Graduate" and "Proficient" (terms which had acquired here a fixed, technical meaning), comparison was directly invited to the more difficult requirements for the M. A. degree, and that, thus, a mark of depreciation was inevitably stamped upon the B. A. degree.

Such was the problem that the Visitors, who desired to act with the utmost conservatism, had to face. After mature deliberation, they established the present B. A. courses, which seemed to them to represent "the amount and sort of training in language, literature, history, philosophy, mathematics, and science, that every educated man should fairly possess." The Visitors specially emphasized that the scope and character of the instruction in some of the courses, at least, for the new B. A. should be essentially different from that required for the M. A. degree, and, to remove all semblance even of stigma, directed that the old nomenclature of "Proficient" should be utterly abolished.

It was ordered that an applicant for the B. A. degree, who had passed his examinations (three-fourths required) in the various departments, should be declared "Graduate in B. A. Latin," "Graduate in B. A. Mathematics," etc.

This does not seem to have been known to your Committee, if the Board may judge from the language of your protest.

But to guard against any possible misapprehension in the future, the Board intends to direct the proper authorities to officially announce in the Catalogue, and elsewhere, the following courses in every Academic School:

1. THE COLLEGIATE COURSE, for the B. A. degree.
2. THE UNIVERSITY COURSE, for the M. A. degree.
3. THE POST-GRADUATE COURSE, for the Ph. D. degree.

Three corresponding diplomas will be granted: (1) *Graduate in the B. A. Course;* (2) *Graduate in the M. A. Course;* (3) *Graduate in the Ph. D. Course.*

As was to be expected, there has been some friction in the adjustment of the details of a scheme so radically different from the old order of things, and, of course, there has been misapprehension as to the scheme itself. The Visitors expected that experience would suggest the advisability of modifications in the original requirements, and such has proved to be the case.

Some options were given in the original (1889) B. A. courses, and it is the purpose of the Board to still further extend the principle of election and to offer additional options in the courses leading up to the B. A. degree. This step is not only in full accord with the aims of the illustrious founder of the University, but, in the judgment of the Visitors, it offers the surest means of securing to our *Alma Mater* in the future a strength and support that have been lacking in the past.

It seems now quite certain that the two B. A.'s of 1891 will be succeeded by eight in 1892, while *fifty-one* students have this session (1891–'92) entered upon courses of study planned to lead up to that degree.

At the same time that the change was made in the requirements for the B. A. degree, the "Committee on Courses of Instruction and the Conduct of Schools" in the Board gave formal notice to the other Visitors that in two years' time, that committee would advise a change in the requirements for the M. A. degree.

Accordingly, at the meeting of the Board of Visitors in July, 1891, the change was recommended, and, after careful discussion, was adopted by the Visitors *without a dissenting voice.*

It is against this latter change that your protest is specially directed. The Visitors must repeat that they have given this paper their most attentive consideration, yet fail to discover in it any argument that has shaken their firm conviction that the change ordered was both wise and imperative.

It has long been known to the members of the Board that a radical modification in the requirements for the M. A. degree has been for years most earnestly desired by a large number (we believe, the majority) of the most thoughtful and intelligent graduates of the University. Not a few of these men have taken the Master's degree here, and have not hesitated to inveigh against the disadvantages of its rigid curriculum.

But it is especially worthy of note that the most emphatic in urging that a radical change should be made, are those M. A. graduates, who have afterwards studied abroad, and who have thus had abundant opportunities for comparing the cast-iron curriculum demanded here with the freedom of election offered by all the famous universities of the Old World.

Thus, since 1889, the Visitors have been informally discussing plans looking to a modification in the requirements for the M. A. degree, seeking, meanwhile, the best judgment of men of wide experience in such matters, who were in every way competent to give weighty and dispassionate advice. This fact is mentioned, that your Committee may be assured that the steps taken by the Board were not taken hastily and unadvisedly, but after the most painstaking investigation and the most deliberate judgment that the Visitors could bring to bear upon such a momentous subject.

It is, doubtless, known to some of the older members of your Committee that the question of "University reform" has been the "burning question" to thoughtful men, at home and abroad, for the past twenty years. During that time, in England and America, the drift has been surely and steadily in one direction—the freedom of election in the higher education, such as had long been granted in the great Continental universities.

Twenty years ago Matthew Arnold struck the key-note of reform in England, when he wrote: "The prime direct aim of instruction is to enable a man to *know himself and the world*. Such knowledge is the only sure basis for action, and this basis it is the true aim and office of instruction to supply. To know himself, a man must know the capabilities and performances of the human spirit; and the value of the humanities, of *Alterthumswissenchaft*, the science of antiquity, is, that it affords for this purpose an unsurpassed source of light and stimulus. Whoever seeks help for knowing himself from knowing the capabilities and performances of the human spirit, will nowhere find a more fruitful object of study than in the achievements of Greece in literature and the arts during the two centuries from the birth of Simonides to the death of Plato. This the humanists have perceived, and the truth of this perception of theirs is the stronghold of their position. But it is also a vital formative knowledge to know the world, the laws that govern nature, and man as a part of nature. This the realists have perceived, and the truth of this perception, too, is inexpugnable."

"Every man is born with aptitudes, which give him access to vital and formative knowledge by one of these roads; either by the road of studying man and his works, or by the road of studying nature and her works. The business of instruction is to seize and *develop these aptitudes.* The great and complete spirits, which have all the aptitudes for both roads of knowledge, are rare. * * * * There should, after a certain point, be no cast-iron course for all scholars, either in humanistic or naturalistic students. *According to his aptitude*, the pupil should be suffered to follow *principally* one branch of either of the two great lines of study; and, above all, to interchange the lines occasionally, following, on the line which is not his own line, such studies as have yet some connection with his own line, or, from any cause whatever, *some attraction for him.*"

The key-note struck by the brilliant Oxford graduate met emphatic support from another illustrious man of letters, who, in his time, had carried off distinguished honors from the University of Cambridge. "I do not say," wrote this great Englishman, "that an attempt may not be made to make an equilibrium between the faculties of the mind, but for any mind to be in its full strength and conscious might, it *must* follow where Nature leads." Much yet remains to be done in the matter of reform, both at Oxford and Cambridge, but these words have borne notable fruit, and the battle, so far as concerns the degree courses, has been practically won by the reformers in each.

That the reforms in our own country, during these twenty years or more, have been many and admirable, no dispassionate observer can deny.

Professor Goodwin, the well-known Greek scholar, in his recent (1891) address on "*The Present and Future of Harvard*," speaking of the reforms inaugurated in that venerable foundation, says: "It is as impossible to imagine an undergraduate of to-day in the college of fifty years ago, or a student of fifty years ago suddenly put into one of our college classes, as to imagine the crowd of passen-

gers, who now go daily from Cambridge to Boston, collected in the square some morning to secure places in the
old stage-coach, which once made its single journey to the
city, or to imagine the venerable Doctor Popkin stepping
calmly out of his door on the West Cambridge road, wav-
ing his historic umbrella to stop an electric car as it goes
whizzing by. This great change in the college is the result
of the elective system of studies which was introduced in
1867. This might be negatively defined as the direct op-
posite of the required system which it superseded. It gave
a great, even an unexpected, stimulus to freedom of every
kind, both in teaching and in studying. It need hardly be
said that the standard of scholarship in every department
was at once raised by this reform. It sprung up of itself
the moment the old pressure was taken off."

It is a distinctive glory, of which no one may rob the
University of Virginia (though many have so sought to
rob her), that she was the first institution among English-
speaking folk to cast off the shackles of the old monastic
narrowness and to allow her students absolute freedom of
election as to studies. But it is equally true, that, while
other great institutions of the first rank in this country,
borrowing from her this elective system, have utilized it
to its fullest logical extent and have emphasized a due
sense of its superlative advantages by offering, as the
bounds of human knowledge have steadily widened, corresponding additional courses (all elective) leading to the
highest academic rewards, she alone has obstinately clung
to a rigid curriculum of requirements for her Master's
degree.

When you say "the requirements for the degree, as it
existed from 1832 to 1860, were substantially the same
as they are *now*," you unconsciously utter a condemna-
tion of "the highest degree conferred in the United States
on undergraduate students" as severe as its most deter-

mined adversaries could possibly frame. It is simply another way of saying, that, while reform in academic degrees has won, the world over, we alone have stood still. It means that, notwithstanding the ever increasing number of studies which, by the deliberate verdict of the ablest and most thoughtful scholars, may fairly claim a place in any scheme of liberal education, a student here, no matter what his commanding aptitudes, no matter how solid and brilliant may be his parts, *must* confine himself to a rigid curriculum, or leave the University without having attained any distinctive mark of academic success.

The old *ante-bellum* M. A., with its curriculum, more or less rigid, was well enough in its day, before the tremendous expansion of the circle of liberal studies. Lord Bacon might, with no undue assumption, declare that he had "taken all human knowledge for his province." But such a declaration to-day, even from "the wisest of mankind," would only provoke a smile of derision.

That degree, when finally established here, represented fairly enough (speaking roughly) the cycle of the old seven *artes liberales* with their "*Trivium*" and "*Quadrivium*"— "the seven liberal arts" of the mediaeval schoolmen. But, as Professor Goodwin aptly says: "These seven arts no longer represent to anybody's mind an encyclopaedic or well-rounded education, though we still gravely make men bachelors and masters of them, while few of us can even remember their seven names. Liberal study has now come to mean whatever is approved by any college authorities as proper study for their students; in short, whatever has the sanction of those who happen to be in power, the *beate possidentes*. Our college authorities (of Harvard) would not let it be said that any one of our three hundred and thirteen courses of study is not liberal study; and it would be hard to draw any consistent line among them which would be in harmony with modern usage."

The history of the M. A. degree of this University, in its various stages of development, as traced by Professor W. M. Thornton in a very striking article, published in the *Religious Herald* for August 6th, 1891, is most instructive reading. As some of your Committee have not, perhaps, seen it, it may be pertinent to draw their attention to facts established by his careful investigations.

He shows that from the original organization of the Academic Department of the University in 1825, with its six independent "Schools" of Ancient Languages, Modern Languages, Mathematics, Natural Philosophy, Natural History, and Moral Philosophy, not a single additional chair was established here down to 1856.

But "by this time the needs of a growing and expanding culture were making themselves felt on all sides," and the Alumni of the University were even then imperatively demanding reform.

Professor Thornton quotes from a sharp arraignment of the shortcomings of the University, published in the *Southern Literary Messenger* for April, 1856, in which the writer, after adverting to the fact mentioned above—that no new chair had been established in the University for the past thirty years—goes on to declare, that "none of its graduates need ever to have heard of botany, or zoology, or political philosophy, not to speak of archaeology, or the fine arts, or theology; that the course in mineralogy and geology consists of but *twelve lectures,* and that in spite of 'the rigorous demands of its examinations,' its Masters of Arts were ushered into the world deaf—as far as their *Alma Mater* cared—to the sublimest harmonies of literature and of nature."

The pressing needs of the University were classified by this writer nearly forty years ago as follows:

1. *A longer period of residence at the University for the students.*

2. *A refusal to admit unprepared youths to matriculation.*

3. Additions to the corps of professors.

4. *A respectable maintenance of the library.*

5. The establishments of scholarships and fellowships.

6. Provision for the study of the literature and philosophy of Christianity.

This fearless and incisive criticism bore immediate fruit.

In May, 1856, the Visitors divided the "School" of Ancient Languages into two distinct "Schools"—(1) Latin; (2) Greek; requested the Faculty to report a plan for the increase of the library; established a chair of "History and Literature": and officially sought the opinion of the Faculty of Medicine as to the need of establishing a course of instruction in Analytical Chemistry. An instructor in this last department was appointed by the Board in 1858. Scarcely had the new professors entered on their duties, when the storm of war burst upon the country, and in a single session "the attendance at the University dropped from 604 men to 66 lads."

"For four years," continues Professor Thornton, "the tide of conflict ebbed and flowed, and when the last battle-flag was furled, the old University found her children dead, or maimed and impoverished, her buildings dilapidated and her faculty scattered. No time was lost, however, in useless lamentation. The faculty re-assembled all of its members who were within reach, pledged their personal credit and fortunes for a loan to rehabilitate the buildings, and reopened the school. Their success was such as to justify the Visitors in filling the chairs which had been vacated by death or resignation. The new current, which, in 1856, bursting the dykes of conservatism, had poured its stream into the channel of her intellectual life, re-appeared with unimpaired force."

It must suffice here to recapitulate in briefest fashion some of the most important results achieved by this devotion and energy on the part of the Faculty and Visitors.

In 1867, a full chair of Applied Chemistry was established, and a laboratory of Analytical Chemistry as well as a museum of Industrial Chemistry, erected. In the same year, a special and separate "Engineering Department" was created.

In 1872, the gift of $100,000 by Samuel Miller of Lynchburg, Virginia, led to the establishment of the "Miller School of Biology and Agriculture," with admirable laboratory equipment for study and research.

In 1879 was established the "Corcoran School of Geology," made possible by the gift of the "Lewis Brooks Museum of Natural History" (costing $80,000) and a gift of $50,000 in money by Mr. Wm. W. Corcoran of Washington, D.C. In the same year, Mr. Corcoran gave $50,000 more, for the endowment of the "Corcoran School of Historical Science" (founded in 1856).

In 1882, was established the "School of Practical Astronomy," which the University owes chiefly to the liberality of Mr. Leander J. McCormick, a resident of Chicago, but native of Virginia, who gave the great twenty-six-inch equatorial telescope, together with sufficient funds for building an astronomical observatory. This new School received a further gift of $25,000 from Mr. Wm. H. Vanderbilt of New York City, as a working fund, which was followed by an endowment fund of $50,000 contributed by the "Society of Alumni."

In the same year, the Visitors created the "School of English."

"Thus," continues Professor Thornton, "at the end of 1890, we see the Academical Department of the University

with its six original Schools increased to thirteen, with
four of the six new Schools completely endowed, with a library enlarged from less than 2,500 volumes to more than
50,000, with a splendid Astronomical Observatory, well-
furnished museums of Industrial Chemistry and Natural
History, and laboratories of Chemistry, Biology, and
Physics—all the rich accumulation of the *last third* of her
corporate life."

After dwelling upon the striking contrast between the
extent of the courses offered at the present time and in
1825, Professor Thornton goes on to say:

"It was not to be expected that this stream of modern
studies, new men and fresh ideas could be injected into the
current of university life without disturbing its tranquil
though somewhat sluggish flow. The miniature battle-
field between the new learning and the old has been the
system of academical degrees. Jefferson himself discarded
the curriculum and contemplated nothing analogous to
the ordinary collegiate degrees. In each School (according
to the original enactments of 1825) 'examinations of the
candidates for honorary distinctions shall be held. At
these examinations shall be given to the highly meritorious
only diplomas of two degrees—the highest of Doctor, the
second of Graduate.' As early as 1831, however, it was
found desirable to reinstate the curriculum in a modified
form, and the degree of Master of Arts was recommended
by the Faculty (July, 1831), and established by the Visitors, the expressed purpose being 'to guide parents in the
selection of studies for their sons, and to lead students to
remain longer at the University.' The Schools included in
this first degree were ancient languages, mathematics, natural philosophy, moral philosophy, and chemistry. In
July, 1832, the visitors ordered that all subsequently ma-
triculated candidates for the degree should pass in two
modern languages, and this provision was first enforced

for the class of '36. In 1846 Anglo-Saxon was expunged from the list of subjects which might be offered for the degree; and in 1859 French and German were defined to be the modern languages required. In 1860 the new School of history and literature was added to the requirements for the degree, but no class of masters was graduated under the enlarged requirements until 1867. From 1867 to 1881 no material change was made in the conditions for graduation. By this time the Schools of analytical chemistry, of biology, and of geology had been established; and in 1882 the Schools of English and practical astronomy were created. The conditions for the master's degree were modified in 1882 so as to make geology and English permissible substitutes for certain courses in the old fixed curriculum. In 1884 a new revision was made of the requirements, and a return to the fixed requirements of 1859 was ordered."

"Such, in its main features, has been the history of this degree. It divides itself into six periods, three falling before the civil war and three after."

"1. In the first period ('32–'35) the requirements were Latin, Greek, mathematics, natural philosophy, moral philosophy, chemistry. The number of masters graduated during this period was 20, the average number of academical students was 86, so that in these four years about 1 student out of 17 received his master's degree."

"2. In the second period ('36–'46) the requirements were enlarged by two modern languages; but inasmuch as any two of the five languages taught in that School could be taken, Anglo-Saxon served as a refuge for the oppressed. The number of masters graduated in these eleven years was 35, the average number of academical students was 98, and the ratio of Masters drops to about 1 out of 31 students.

"3. In the third period ('47–'61) the requirements were rendered still more rigid by the exclusion of Anglo-Saxon from the elective list. The number of masters graduated in fifteen years was 90; the average number of academical students was 258; and the ratio drops still further to about 1 master out of 43 students."

"4. In the fourth period ('67-'81) the screw receives another turn. French and German are required of all masters, and the School of history and literature is added to the conditions for the degree. In the fifteen years there are 53 masters, with an average of 218 academical students; the ratio drops again to about 1 master out of 62 students."

"This steady progression—17, 31, 43, 72—tells its own story and needs no comment. Each figure has a voice, and could preach a sermon. The faculty and the visitors, continually tampering with the degree, show a blind consciousness that 'there is something rotten in the State of Denmark,' but seem to blink the issue and ignore the fact that their original curriculum is ready to perish from its own weight and aridity."

"5. In the fifth period ('82-'84) the first gleam of light is thrown over this desolating picture. It is the Golden Age of the Master's degree. The limited freedom of election permitted by the new regulations attracts a larger number of applicants."

"In three years 25 masters are graduated, with an average of 164 academical students; and the ratio rises from 1 in 62 to 1 master in less than 20 students."

"6. In the sixth period ('85 to the present) we return to the [Cast] Iron Age. The requirements are diminished by the excision of historical science and by discarding the review examinations formerly held, but at the same time all freedom of election is taken away, and we go back to the rigid curriculum of 1859. In the seven years 30 masters are graduated, with an average attendance of 200 academical students, and the ratio drops again from 1 in 20 to 1 in 47. *Of the entire thirty but three are known to the*

writer who have devoted themselves to the advancement
of any branch of learning taught to them here. The re-
maining 90 per cent. have given themselves to other studies
or have forsaken the pursuit of letters and science."

"It seems scarcely necessary, after this array of facts,
which should carry conviction to any candid mind, to cor-
roborate the evidence they furnish by comparing the time
required to take this degree in the several periods above.
It is well known that it has been the aim of our best Vir-
ginian schools not to prepare their boys for the lowest
class in the University and send them up for a full scholas-
tic term of four or more years, but, on the contrary, to
prepare them for the highest classes and reduce their residence at the University to a minimum. With this in mind,
let it suffice simply to state that in the twenty years, from
1840 to 1861, there were 17 two-year masters, and in the
twenty-five years from 1867 to 1891, but one; and again,
that in the *ante-bellum* period there were 94 masters with
a residence of three years or less against 51 with a residence of four years or more, whereas in the *post-bellum*
period the inequality is reversed, there being 35 with a residence of three years or less against 73 with a residence of
four years or more."

"Impressed with a sense of the necessity of action, the
visitors have recently taken the question of degrees into
consideration anew, and have blazed out a path different
from any heretofore trodden. A bachelor's degree has been
established of great freedom and flexibility, little restriction
being placed upon the student's election of studies beyond
the fact that no one of the five great departments of learning—ancient languages, modern languages, mathematics,
natural and physical sciences, and historical and philosophical sciences—may be altogether neglected. The candidate for the master's degree, under the new rules, must
first take his B. A. and then pursue *advanced university*

courses in four Schools of the academical department—as, for example, in Latin, Greek, moral philosophy and modern languages; or in mathematics, natural philosophy, theoretical and practical astronomy, and modern languages. The grouping of the Schools, the extent of the requirements demanded in each, and the character of the tests is left to the faculty. But on the new degrees there is incised—deep, clear, and ineffacable—the principle of FREEDOM OF ELECTION. Let us hope that these pioneers, like many others guided by Providence, may prove to have 'builded even better than they knew,' and that there will issue from the old University a constantly growing procession of young men trained thoroughly in her lecture-rooms for the vocations of modern life, and worthy in *number*, as well as in *character*, of her dowry and position."

This "principle of THE FREEDOM OF ELECTION" has been, in truth, the guiding principle, kept steadily in view by the Visitors in the changes they have seen fit to make.

We have quoted thus at length from Professor Thornton's admirable paper, because, as indicated above, we believe that the facts stated in that paper must be unknown to a considerable number of your Committee. Had the facts been fully laid before them, we feel confident that not a few, at least, among the signers of the protest would have seen the necessity of no longer ignoring in the schemes for academic degrees some of the most important subjects of human study.

To the Visitors it seemed plain that to longer insist on the narrow old curriculum meant not conservatism but ossification, and that, in recognizing in the degrees of the future a greater freedom of election, they were not only taking a step imperatively demanded, if this institution were to be kept abreast of the great universities at home and abroad, but that they were for the first time giving full expression to the essential purpose of the founder of the University, who in intelligent apprehension of the true methods of higher education was fully fifty years ahead of his times.

It is, perhaps, natural that young men who have so recently passed successfully "the dread ordeal" of the old curriculum requirements for the M. A. degree, shall indulge in Cassandra warnings as to the direful results that must ensue from the "radical" changes ordered by the Visitors. It is only pertinent to say that their fears are not shared by the Visitors, who for the past three years have been carefully considering every objection urged in the protest, not to mention others, which find no expression in that paper. .

There have been graduated altogether *two hundred and fifty-three* Masters of Arts from this University, of whom one hundred and forty-five took the degree prior to the war, and one hundred and eight since. You present to us a protest signed by but thirty-five of these Masters, and by eight students "applicants for the degree." Of these *thirty-five* Masters, *twenty-nine* have taken the degree *within the past ten years*, and there can be no offense in observing that, with *perhaps* two exceptions, not one of the twenty-nine has had any adequate opportunity for thoughtful comparison of the system familiar to him here with the systems that obtain in the other great institutions of this country and of Europe. As to the value of the opinions of the "applicants for the degree," the same observation may be repeated, and the Visitors have not failed to note that one of these young gentlemen, immediately after signing a protest, which declared that the changes made would "ruin" the present "honorable position" of the M. A. degree, applied in writing to the Board to be allowed to take the degree under the new conditions in 1892, one year before those conditions were to go into effect. It is needless to say that the Board had no authority to grant this extraordinary request, but the application was none the less significant as to the depth of his conviction on the subject.

On the other hand, since the publication of the orders of the Board authorizing the changes in the requirements for the M. A. and B. A. degrees, the Visitors have received the most emphatic assurances of approval from many of the most distinguished "graduates" and Masters of the University—men of wide and mature experience, who have had abundant opportunity of weighing dispassionately the merits of the old curriculum with those offered by freedom of election.

In your protest you state: "We consider that the degree of M. A. of the University of Virginia is the highest degree conferred in the United States on undergraduate students. Such it is acknowledged to be by all who are competent to form an opinion entitled to value." After quoting Professor J. H. Wright, of Harvard, as to the "singularly honorable position" of the M. A. degree here, you continue: "We submit that the peculiar distinction *universally* accorded this degree, as it now exists, is of inestimable value to the University, that its reputation is worth preserving, that a radical change in the *nature* of its requirements will ruin its present 'honorable position,' and necessitate the acquisition of a new reputation, that any change approximating our degree to those of other institutions in America will destroy its individuality and impair its usefulness."

There must be so wide a diversity of opinion touching some of the points so confidently stated in the above paragraph, that the Visitors need scarcely enter upon any discussion of them. It may be pertinent, however, to remind you that Professor Wright, who is undoubtedly a competent judge in such matters, is one of the most strenuous advocates of freedom of election in academical courses leading up to degrees. But waiving that as a minor point, there is surely nothing in the changes made by the Board in the requirements for the M. A. degree that can in any way tend to diminish the high respect which, it is claimed, is "universally accorded this degree."

The work in the present senior classes of the University is fully one year ahead of the best American collegiate work. This is distinctively true as to Latin, Greek, Mathematics, Natural Philosophy, Moral Philosophy, Astronomy and Biology. It is true in spirit of the Analytical Chemistry, considered as an extension of the General Chemistry. It is, in the main, true of French and German. It is true also of the work in Mineralogy and Geology, although this work, as is the work in English and Historical Science, is divided according to subject and not according to grade.

Thus if there should be no further development in the courses offered in these "Schools," it is entirely safe to say that the M. A. degree of this University would still represent more solid work than is now required for the M. A. degree of any other American institution of learning. [See *Harvard Catalogue for 1891*, p. 262; *Yale Catalogue for 1891*, p. 103; *Cornell Catalogue for 1891*, p. 162.]

The fear, then, which you express that "the present 'honorable position' of the degree will be ruined," seems to the Visitors entirely groundless, and it is noteworthy, as confirmatory of their confidence in the wisdom of the changes made, that a majority of the Faculty of the University approve cordially of these changes, and that of the *four* Masters of Arts filling academic chairs in their *Alma Mater*, three of these Masters (all trained abroad and so competent to compare the old and new systems) ardently favor the reforms inaugurated by the Board. Your protest continues: "The Master of Arts degree has for sixty years been the distinctive feature of this institu-

tion and the University guarantees the scholarship of all
who bear it; as long as it is given, the fame of the University must largely depend on the acquirements of its Masters. A host of men have left these walls bearing this
honorable title, who justly regard it as the outward indication of high attainments in the field of literature and
science."

That the Master's degree "has for sixty years been" the
distinctive feature "of this institution" is alas! true, and
the Visitors must say emphatically that they cannot but
deem it a great misfortune to the University that such
should have been the case. It has gradually attained here
such an exaggerated importance as has rendered it impossible that any other academic degree should flourish at all.
The whole tone of your protest reflects a view which, the
Visitors believe, has been distinctly harmful to the best interests of the University. Apparently, it is tacitly assumed
that the University was made for the Master's degree and
not that the Master's degree was made for the University.
"*The* degree," as it is called, has utterly dwarfed every
other sort of academical distinction, and the tendency of
the overshadowing importance attached to it, has more
and more during the years since the war been the reverse
of healthful. It has not been to bring the University as a
centre of teaching into direct contact with the life of the
State. It has not been to foster what should be the chief
function of a great institution of learning, to-wit: the
broad and liberal education of *the great body of students*,
who, whether they eventually become lawyers, physicians,
clergymen, or, as merchants, go into trade, should leave
her walls amply equipped to play their part worthily in
raising the general tone of intelligence and refinement
wherever it might please God to call them. On the contrary, it has long seemed to many of the most devoted of
our graduates, that the tendency has been more and more

surely in the direction of dissociating the University from the life of the State, in narrowing her capacity for practical usefulness, and in restricting her chief function to that of a mere nursery for specialists and technical scholars.

That any student should be enabled, if he so desire, to receive here the training of a specialist, that technical education of the most advanced and thorough kind should be offered in all departments, no one denies. But it is the first duty of such an institution as this to provide for the *sound* and liberal education of the greatest number—to make its main degree one that no fool or idler can take as a matter of course, yet such a degree as no student of fair ability need despair of attaining within three years. In other words, it is the duty of such an institution to see to it that the best interests of the many are not sacrified to those of the few.

There were enrolled last session in the Academic Department of the University two hundred and forty-two students, and of this number just *three* men took "*the* degree." Commenting on this startling state of affairs, Professor R. H. Dabney says in one of the many admirable articles contributed by him to the public press: "Of the 479 students at the University last session, how many took this degree? Why just *three*. Nor does it often happen that the annual 'host' numbers more than five or six. Surely, there is something rotten in the state of Denmark if 'the fame of the University' really 'depends' upon the acquirements of half a dozen men in five hundred. I am far from wishing for the day when any degree of the University shall be awarded to nine-tenths of those whose names are enrolled in the catalogue; but if three men are to carry off all the glory, while 476 are left in outer darkness, the time for a revolution is come. Not one of these three would claim for a moment, I am sure, that they alone among the students of 1890–'91 possess sufficient knowledge and brains to add to the University's fame. It is perfectly true, however, that many a clever and ambitious man leaves the University with far less knowledge and mental training than would be the case if the University offered him a degree that could be obtained without the mind-crushing process of cram, which so many employ to obtain the present M. A. The fact that of all the students enrolled in the last catalogue only 203 had spent more than one year at the University, only 74 more than two years, and only 27 more than three years, is a startling fact." After stating his reasons for believing that this state of affairs is by no means due to the poverty of our people, he continues: "Many causes may coöperate to drive students from our University, but none is more potent, I believe, than the fact, that being told that the M. A. degree is the chief glory of the place, and that other degrees are mere high-school affairs, unworthy of a serious thought; seeing that only one in a hundred succeeds in getting this degree, and seeing also that even that one gets it at the cost of suffering and pain, many a student becomes discouraged at the start, and, after performing his work for one year in a half-hearted way, leaves the University in disgust. The truth is that the M. A. degree in its present shape is an incubus upon the University, weighing her down and driving men from her walls."

These are the deliberate words of a Professor in this institution, who is both a master of Arts of this University, and a Doctor of Philosophy of a famous German one.

How entirely the B. A. degree—which should be the popular degree of this University, as it is of all the great universities of the English-speaking world—has been dwarfed into insignificance by the exaggerated importance paid here to the M. A. degree, is abundantly proved by the following statistics: Since the foundation of the University sixty-seven years ago, there have been altogether but 81

Bachelors of Arts, an average of little over one a year; *forty* took this degree prior to the war, and *forty-one* since. Again, of the 40 *ante-bellum* B. A.'s, 11, later on, secured the M. A.; of the 41 *post-bellum* B. A.'s, 23, later on, took the M. A. In other words, only 18 men during the past 25 years have taken the B. A. degree for its own sake, the others having taken it as part of their M. A. course. Of these 18, one is a candidate for M. A. this session.

Contrast with this deplorable state of things the fact already mentioned (in the earlier part of this paper) that *fifty-one* men have this year entered upon courses of study planned to lead up to the B. A. degree.

" *Each figure has a voice and could preach a sermon.*"

Again you say: " The *great renown* in which our M. A. is held both at home and abroad, rests upon two pillars; the *immense* field over which it extends and the high standard of attainments necessary for success in each department of knowledge. Take away either of these supports, and the other is not sufficient to hold us up; the first bears the fame of our degree for a liberal education, the last carries our reputation for high attainments *in all departments of such an education.* Without the one, the M. A. becomes merely a special degree, showing perhaps high development on one or two lines, but is no longer the synonym for a well-rounded and polished gentleman— without the other, our degree men are *Dilettantes* (sic), possessed of that most baneful of all acquirements—a little learning."

That the M. A. degree of this University has always been the most difficult undergraduate degree to attain in this country is perfectly true. That it represents more actual work within its curriculum than any other American M. A. degree is equally true, and the Visitors are well aware that the training in the seven Schools required for graduation has been most severe. That it has enjoyed in the past "at home" (that is, in the Southern States) a great, nay, an exaggerated reputation, none may deny. But, it is equally true that the degree is but little known in the North, and not at all known in Europe. A large majority of even educated Americans possess but little idea of the requirements for academic degrees at Oxford and Cambridge, at Dublin and Edinburgh, and fewer still can distinguish between the value of a degree granted by one German university and that granted by another. When we consider the vast number of "universities" in this comparatively new country of ours, it cannot seem unnatural that the ignorance "abroad" of the value of American degrees should be distinctly greater than our ignorance of foreign degrees, and to say that the M. A. degree of the University of Virginia is "held in great renown abroad," however pleasing it may be to our self-complacency, is a statement scarcely justified by the facts.

One of the greatest of English critics, a man who is highly regarded in his own country as being specially conversant with American affairs, alluded several years ago in a volume of his collected "Essays" to the University of Virginia as "a military school, situated at Lexington, Virginia, of which Gen'l Ro. E. Lee was President." This is merely mentioned as "a case in point."

As to "the immense field of knowledge over which it extends," Prof. Dabney has, it seems to the Visitors, pointed out in most trenchant fashion the rhetorical exaggeration of this claim. He has pointed out that the old degree contained no Astronomy, "a science marvellous for its accuracy and unsurpassed in the grandeur of its theme"—that it contained no Biology, "that fertile science, which more than all others within the past thirty years has revolutionized philosophies and religious thought"—that it contained no Geology, "that science, which traces back into the fabulous past the history of the earth, its strata, and the countless fossil forms therein contained," that it contains no History, no Italian, no Spanish, most astounding of all, in view of the claim of "the immense field of knowledge over which it extends," no instruction in our own tongue, the tongue of Chaucer and Spenser, of Shakspere and Milton, of Swift and Bolingbroke, of Wordsworth and Tennyson. "Far be it from me," exclaims Dr. Dabney, "to claim that all these subjects are necessary to a liberal education. But I would ask my brother Masters of Arts to prove that Chemistry strengthens the mind more than Astronomy, French more than Italian, Schiller more than Shakspere."

The truth seems to be that, while the "field" cannot be said to be "immense," if we regard the wide and ever-widening range of liberal studies, it was entirely too "immense," in view of the fact, that in some of the Schools the training appears to have been steadily drifting into technical work of a semi-specialistic character. To say that a man is receiving a specialistic or quasi-specialistic training in seven widely different directions, is to say that he will most probably never become a real specialist in any one of the seven. The old M. A. has come to be regarded more and more of recent years as a degree specially adapted to equip a man for the profession of teaching. Yet, when these graduates have elected any special line in the *higher education*, they have soon discovered that, by reason of dissipating their energies in working on lines having no connection with one another, they were in no true sense specialists, and that they must study further in some foreign university (or in the Johns Hopkins, at home) in order to hold a reputable place among the best instructors in the department of learning elected.

Advanced college-work with a strong element of specialism infused, is not, it is needless to say, necessarily "Uni-

versity work." The work in the ancient languages, for
instance, may be true "university work," and yet not be
specialistic work of the strictest character. That some of
the work will be of a specialistic nature is, doubtless, true,
but the methods of instruction will not be so rigorously
scientific as the pure and simple specialistic work required
in the Ph. D. course. To quote Matthew Arnold again
(and no more competent authority can be appealed to in
the case), "Scientific instruction, university instruction
really begins when the degree of Bachelor (*bas chevalier*,
knight of low degree) is taken, and preparation for master-
ship in any line, or for doctorship (fitness to teach it)
commences."

After naming the seven Schools comprised in the curriculum for the old M. A., you exclaim: "Who can say that
a deep insight into all of these is not essential to a liberal
education? Who would say that more is required?" We
believe that a great number of very able men would say
both things, and it is to be noted that you yourselves think
that something more is required, for you close your protest
by saying, "We agree heartily that some option should be
allowed, and to that extent that the degree be broadened."

Again you assert: "The Master of Arts degree provided
for by the action of the Board is either a post-graduate
degree or an undergraduate degree of lower standard than
the old one; the Bachelor's degree is made a prerequisite,
and the Master's degree may then be attained by graduation in any four Schools approved by the Faculty; if it be
meant by this requirement that no one can get an M. A.
unless he has graduated in four Schools after getting a B.
A., the character of man who will, in future, apply for our
distinctive degree will be changed; there are few undergraduate students so well prepared that they cannot profitably devote their time to the Senior classes of the various
Schools; to such students the B. A. opens no new course

of study, but merely a review of his high-school work. As a manifest consequence of this fact, this alternative presents itself: either the high-school graduate will seek other fields of study, and the degree will be neglected, or since the amount of preparation for the B. A. course is much less, students of poor attainments and very young years will present themselves, and instead of men of 18 or 20 entering the University, lads of 15 or 16, who may prefer to get their Academic training at this place instead of at school, will come in; and since the entire freedom of restraint, which is granted to men here, could not in justice be allowed to those who would be but boys in years, our whole system must necessarily be changed and the surveillance and restraint of high school and college be introduced."

The Visitors have, each and all, read over this paragraph of your protest with the most careful attention and are reluctantly forced to admit that they cannot grasp in any degree the meaning of a considerable portion of it. Waiving that portion, they must reiterate that you entirely misapprehend the nature of the charges made, if you suppose that there is to be any lowering of the standard required in the Schools for the old degree. On the contrary, they are firmly convinced, as already stated, that, with a sound B. A. degree as a prerequisite for the new M. A. degree, the courses of instruction for the latter degree must, of necessity, be gradually broadened and advanced, and the "renown" of the degree be enhanced in the eyes of a majority of the Alumni, as resting on a more intelligent foundation. The Master of Arts of the future should be more truly a Master than the Master of the past, for he will already have received in his B. A. course a sound general knowledge of those subjects deemed essential as the basis of a liberal education, and, in addition, will have received a wider and more thorough training in those related studies which his special aptitudes have caused him to elect for this advanced work. "I cannot emphasize too strongly," says Professor Goodwin, "that the chief merit of the present elective system is not that it lets students study what they like and avoid what they dislike, but that it opens to all a higher and wider range of study in every field; in short, it has made really high scholarship possible."

As to the fear that "students of poor attainments and very young years will present themselves," the following passage from the last "*Report of the President of Harvard College*" should suffice to allay that apprehension: "It is noticeable that no one now enters under 16 and very few over 21 years of age; but that the average age at admission, which reached 19 years ten years ago, has not diminished during the last decade." Significant too is the following vote of the Overseers of Harvard (June 4th, 1890): "Voted, that, in the opinion of the Board of Overseers, the present average age of admission of the Freshman class, about 19 years, is undesirably high and that the actual age of admission might with advantage be reduced, so that, for the great majority of the class, it should be between 17 and 18 years."

It should be further remembered that the requirements for the B. A. degree at Harvard are not so severe as those established here by the Visitors, and that in the case of students from Virginia "the Faculty of the University are required *by law* to be satisfied by actual examination of the applicant or by a certificate from some college or preparatory school, that he has made such proficiency in the branch of study which he proposes to pursue as will enable him to avail himself of the advantages afforded by the University" (See *Catalogue of Univ. of Va.*, 1890–'91, p. 48).

The protest continues: "If the language of the Board be

interpreted to mean that any man, who has graduated in four Schools and obtained proficiency in a sufficient number of classes to entitle him to the degree of Bachelor of Arts will receive his M. A., we submit that the standard of the University's distinctive degree, and, therefore, the standard of the University, has been lowered; for the present requirements, there would be substituted a requirement of four proficiencies and four graduations. This provision that the Schools elected are to be approved by the Faculty must be a dead letter, since the discretion given to them is an arbitrary discretion, without any rule to guide them, and, therefore, they could not fairly exercise it against a B. A., who had graduated in four Schools. According to this interpretation a well-prepared man could with ease accomplish the work required for the M. A. degree in two years, whereas, at Harvard, it was only after long and mature consideration that the B. A. course was shortened from four to three years."

As regards the first portion of this paragraph, enough has already been said, we trust, to show that the language of the Board has been entirely misinterpreted regarding the scope and character of the work required in the B. A. courses, and that no further space need be wasted on that point. Touching the statement that the discretion given the Faculty as to approving the Schools elected "must be a dead letter," because that discretion is an arbitrary discretion, the Visitors have only to say that the opinion so confidently expressed by the young gentlemen of your Committee is directly opposed to the opinion reached by the mature judgment of the most experienced scholars the world over, who have devoted themselves to the problems involved in University reform.

The Visitors have the fullest confidence in the experience and sound judgment of the Faculty touching the matter, and it is precisely because the discretion granted them is free of all conditions, that it possesses any practical value. We may all be sure that they will in the future, as in the past, be sufficiently jealous of the reputation of the University to allow no group of studies to be offered for the M. A. degree not fully representing the high requirements for the new degree.

As the fact may be unknown to your Committee, we will further state this discretionary power granted by the Visitors is precisely that which obtains at Oxford, Cambridge, Harvard, Yale, Cornell, &c. As you instance Harvard in the above paragraph, we draw your attention to p. 262 of the *Harvard Catalogue for* 1890–'91: "The Faculty of Arts and Sciences will recommend for the degree of Master ' of Arts candidates otherwise properly qualified, who, after taking the Bachelor's degree, shall pursue for at least one year at the University a course of liberal study *approved by the Faculty*, and shall pass with high credit an examination on that course." [See also *Catalogue of Yale University*, p. 115; *Cornell*, p. 161.]

Such is also the plan pursued at the Johns Hopkins University in regard to courses offered for the Ph. D. degree.

As to whether "a well-prepared man" could take the new M. A. in two years, certainly the feat is possible; but, in view of the fact that no less than 17 men took the *antebellum* M. A. (which your Committee allows was "a good degree") in that time, and that even the same *tour de force* has been successfully accomplished since the war within the same period of time, we do not see that "the great renown" of your "distinctive degree" is likely to be endangered by such exceptional performance.

That even the best prepared men could take the new degree "with ease" in that time, we do not for one moment believe. This assumption we must regard as based more on a consciousness of unusual mental power on the part of some of your Committee than on a mature survey of the average intellectual ability of the young men who commonly apply here for the degree.

"Let me ask these gentlemen," says Dr. Dabney in the article already quoted, "who consider this so easy a task, whether they are aware that of all the Academic students (245) of the session of 1889–'90, only 89 graduated even in *one* subject, only 32 in more than one, and only 6 in more than two. I believe that the new degree which does not require a man to plough through the senior classes of those subjects which he loathes, will serve to make the students more hopeful, and that larger 'tickets' will be made in future than hitherto. But with the above figures in view, he seems to me a most self-confident man, who thinks he could make four graduations and five proficiencies in two years and mark you, 'with ease.' Suppose he choose Latin, Greek, Mathematics, and Moral Philosophy for his advanced work. Then, even if he make the direful 'Green Ticket' (Latin, Greek, and Math.) the first year, he will have to perform the work in *seven classes, with twenty lectures a week, the second year*, in order to obtain the degree."

Following the above paragraph (already commented on), you say: "According to either interpretation a man might be an M. A. of the University of Virginia without having more than *a slight knowledge of Latin*: he might be an M. A. without having even heard that there is such a thing as Calculus, or without knowing a principle of Psychology or a law of Logic. He might receive his degree without having shown any greater knowledge of foreign languages than just enough to enable him to pass his examinations in the Intermediate Classes in Latin and French; he might be wholly ignorant of Chemistry or of Pysics. Is it becoming the dignity of the University to confer its highest degree upon one who has shown no scholarly knowledge of the languages, ancient or modern, and who may not have stood a single examination in Pure Mathematics? It would seem a misnomer to confer the degree of Master of Arts on one who may have confined himself entirely in his senior studies to Science or to Literature, and who has passed through his lower studies under a depreciated standard. He is master in only half of the field; hitherto the title has been conferred only on those who had graduated in the highest classes in each of the prescribed Schools; it is neither right nor just for the University to mislead the public by conferring its time-honored degree on men of inferior attainments."

The Visitors have no need to be taught their duty as to what is "right" and "just for the University" to do, nor are they likely to "mislead the public," of which they naturally have a wider knowledge than have the young gentlemen of your Committee.

But let us consider the above statements separately.

Certainly no man can graduate in the B. A. Latin course, as prescribed by the Visitors, "without having more than a *slight knowledge of Latin.*" It was prescribed that he should read a far greater volume of Latin than has heretofore been the case in the University, that he should possess a sound knowledge of Latin syntax, and that he should pass satisfactory examinations in "a thorough course of Roman History and Roman Literature" (see orders of the Board, February 9th, 1889). But, while it was never, of course, designed that a student should not evidence an intelligent grasp of the essential and fundamental principles of Latin Syntax, and that a proper knowledge of such principles should not be insisted on in the daily exegesis of the authors read in class, and should not be fully tested by his capacity and readiness in Latin prose composition, the Visitors, convinced that no literature, ancient or modern, can be satisfactorily studied from the philological side alone, distinctly proposed that the weight of instruction in the B. A. course should lie in the direction of bringing the student into closer contact and familiarity with the great Roman writers *in mass*, and especially in' opening up to him a wider view of ancient life, literature, and manners, than can ever be attained from a purely philological study of the niceties of the language. It must be remembered that the young men who come up to the University from our best schools, have been trained for years in these syntactical niceties of Latin and Greek Syntax, and it is only proper and reasonable, that, when these students enter upon the broader and freer life here, they should find broader and freer courses of study than those they have known at school—that all, save those who purpose to become teachers (a small minority), should be offered, *not* a "harder" course in the same line of study as that they have been pursuing in the best high schools, but a course comprising a wide and intelligent survey of the social, political, and intellectual life of the ancient world. Young men, who have not this syntactical training, should be excluded from these classes by the examinations now made 'obligatory by law.

"But many people," says Matthew Arnold, "have even convinced themselves that the preliminary philological discipline is so extremely valuable as to be an end in itself; and, similarly that the mathematical discipline preliminary to a knowledge of nature is so extremely valuable as to be an end in itself. It seems to me that those who profess this conviction do not enough consider the quantity of knowledge inviting the human mind, and the importance to the human mind of really getting to it. No preliminary discipline is to be pressed at the risk of keeping minds from getting at the main matter, a knowledge of themselves and the world. Some minds have such a special aptitude for philology, or for pure mathematics, that their access to vital knowledge and their genuine intellectual life lies in and through these studies; but for *one* whose *natural* access to vital knowledge is by these paths, there will be *ten* whose natural access to it is through literature, philosophy, history, or through some one or more of the natural sciences. No doubt, it is indispensable to have exact habits of mind, and mathematics and grammar are excellent for the promotion of these habits; and Latin, besides having so large a share in so many modern languages, offers a grammar which is the best of all grammars for this promotion. Here are valid reasons for making every schoolboy learn some Latin and some mathematics, but not for turning the preliminary matter into the principal, and sacrificing every aptitude except that for the science of language and of pure mathematics. But it is sometimes said that only through close philological studies and the close practice of Greek and Latin composition, can *Alterthumswissenchaft* itself, the science of the ancient world, be truly reached. It is said to be only through these that we get really to know Greek and Latin literature. For all practical purposes this proposition is untrue, and its untruth may be easily tested. Ask a good Greek scholar, in the ordinary English acceptation of that term, who at the same time knows a modern literature—let us say the French literature—well, whether he feels himself to have most seized the spirit and power of French literature, or of Greek literature. Undoubtedly he has most seized the spirit and power of French literature, simply because he has read so very much more of it. But if, instead of reading work after work of French literature, he had read only a few works on parts of works in it, and had given the rest of his time for study to the sedulous practice of French composition, and to minutely learning the structure and laws of the French language, then he would know the French literature much as he knows the Greek; he might write very creditable French verses, but he would have

seized the spirit and power of French literature not half
so much as he has seized them at present. An immense
development of grammatical studies, and an immense use
of Latin and Greek composition, take so much of the pupil's time, that in nine cases out of ten he has not any
sense at all of Greek and Latin literature as *literature*,
and ends his studies without getting any. His verbal
scholarship and his composition is pretty sure in after life
to drop, and then all his Greek and Latin is lost. Greek
and Latin *literature*, if he had ever caught the notion of
them, would have been far more likely to stick by him.
* * * I am convinced that of the hundreds whom our
present system tries without distinction to bring into contact with *Alterthumswissenchaft* through composition
and philology almost alone, *the immense majority* would
have a far better chance of being brought into vital contact with it through literature, and by treating the study
of Greek and Latin as we treat our French or Italian, or
German studies. In other words, the number of persons
with aptitudes for being carried to vital knowledge by the
literary, or historical, or philosophical, or artistic sense—
to each of which senses we give a chance by treating Greek
and Latin as literature, and not as mere scholarship—is
infinitely greater than the number of those whose aptitudes are for composition and philology."

Such is the weighty utterance on this subject of a man,
who, apart from his prodigious learning in both ancient
and modern languages, was the best informed man of our
times in regard to the methods and requirements of the
secondary and higher education in England, France, and
Germany.

But to return to the *minutiæ* of your protest.

As to French, it was never proposed that "Junior," nor
yet "Intermediate French," should be the measure of requirement for the B. A. course in that department. The

details of the matter were left to the professor, with the understanding that the work in B. A. French and German should be about the equivalent of the work formerly required for "graduation" in the *ante-bellum* School of Modern Languages. Advanced courses in historical grammar and in Romance and Teutonic philology were to find their place in the work for the higher degrees.

True, "a man might be an M. A." without having graduated on Calculus, and it *might* be within the range of possibilities that he might never even have "heard of" it, seeing that a prominent member of your Committee has forwarded to the Board, along with the protest, an article written by himself, in which he confesses that he "hasn't an idea what the course in Practical Astronomy may be." He further asks, "Who has?" As the School of Astronomy in the University has long been known as the "School of Practical Astronomy," the head of that School most probably has an idea on the subject, and it would seem that any man holding this degree of "great renown" ought, at least, to have "heard" of such well-known textbooks as "Loomis's *Practical Astronomy*," "Chauvenet's Spherical and *Practical* Astronomy," or "Pearson's Introduction to *Practical* Astronomy."

True, "a man might be an M. A. without knowing a principle of Psychology or a law of Logic," but so, under the old order, he might be an M. A. without knowing a principle of the science of Geology, or a single one of the fundamental laws of plant and animal life as taught in the science of Biology. As to Chemistry and Physics, he must, under the new order, know one or the other, while under the old curriculum, he might never "even have heard" of Magna Charta or the French Revolution.

"He might be an M. A." with no minute knowledge of classical philology, but, surely, that is far less a defect in the education of "a well-rounded and polished gentle-

man" than that he should never have given proof that he
had read a line of Shakspere and Tennyson, of Fielding
and Thackeray.

It does not seem improbable to the Visitors, that, when
you gave utterance to the assertion that "it would seem
a misnomer to confer the degree of *Master of Arts*" on
one who may have confined himself entirely in his senior
studies to science *or* to literature," your committee was
ignorant of the fact that this is precisely what is done by
the great universities of Germany. The degree given at
Berlin and Leipzig, at Göttingen and Bonn to students
who successfully pass their examinations "in science or
in literature," is "*Philosophiæ Doctor et Artium Mag-
ister,*" both degrees being conferred at once. Surely, the
University of Virginia may dub *Master of Arts* those who
have pursued successfully an advanced course on one of
these two great lines of study, even as these great Continental universities do, and yet not "mislead the public."
The same is true at Harvard (See *Harvard Catalogue,*
1890–91, p. 222).

As the German student, who has successfully passed, at
the close of his "gymnasium" career, his "Leaving Examination" ("*Abiturientenexamen*"—the equivalent of our
B. A.) is allowed on entering the University the widest
field of choice as to the line of study he may wish to pursue leading up to the "distinctive degree"in that country,
so here on B. A. should be allowed the same freedom when
he enters upon his advanced work. A like freedom of
choice is given in France to those who enter the university
with the "*Épreuve du Baccalauréat*" from the "*Haut
Lycée.*"

Your protest further says: "In the proposed scheme of
the new M. A., it is possible to become a Master of Arts
of the University of Virginia with absolutely no knowledge of Greek, &c. The proposed change is a blow to the

study of Greek, which must certainly result in serious consequences. * * * * We would enter a respectful protest against the University lending a helping hand to what foreshadows the death of the study of Greek at the University. A large percentage of those who take the senior class in Greek are at present those who have as their ultimate goal the Master's degree, and if an avowedly easier road is opened to them, many will desert the field of Greek altogether."

It is almost needless to say that the Visitors do not in the least share these gloomy forebodings. The three men, who are to-day, perhaps, the most competent to give a really valuable and unbiased opinion on this question, are all heartily in favor of making Greek an elective in degree courses. It is an open secret that Dr. B. L. Gildersleeve, confessedly the greatest Hellenist in America, whose teaching here for twenty years raised the whole standard of wide and exact scholarship throughout the South, and whose subsequent contributions to classical philology have revolutionized the old methods of Greek study throughout the North, favors the action of the Board in this matter. His successor here in the Greek chair, Professor Thomas R. Price, himself a brilliant Master of Arts, and afterward a devoted disciple of the great Curtius, is also an ardent advocate of the change from the old hard-and-fast curriculum to a free election of lines of study leading up to the M. A. degree. Can any one credit for a single moment that these two illustrious scholars, whose fame is indissolubly bound up with that of this University, whose devotion to the best interests of the University is unquestioned, and who know as much of her past and present needs as any two living men, would favor any change that, as you confidently assert, "foreshadows the death of the study of Greek in the University?"

If Greek be all that it is claimed to be—if the Greek language still remains the immortal canon, in poetry and prose, for exquisite beauty and precision in the expression of human thought by human speech—if the literature of Greece be, in truth, one of the noblest instruments of intellectual culture known to men—(and the Visitors beg leave to say that they believe both claims to be well founded)—then we may all of us be sure that the study of the Greek language and the Greek literature will not die out here, nor at any of the other great universities in our land.

As regards "the large percentage" of those who only study Greek here because their "ultimate goal" is the Master's degree, the quicker they drop the study of Greek and take up some other line of study, for which they may possibly have a special aptitude, the better for them, for the University, and for the Master's degree. They may, indeed, secure a diploma in Greek, but they can never become Greek scholars in any true sense, and a degree so taken will not improbably prove "the ultimate goal" of their whole career.

The third distinguished scholar, who favors making Greek an elective in all degree courses, is Dr. William W. Goodwin, Eliot Professor of Greek Literature in Harvard University. For thirty-five years he has taught Greek at Harvard, and has had almost unparalleled opportunities for contrasting the old and new systems. "If," says he, "I have not looked at the question solely or chiefly from the classical point of view, and considered merely what seemed to be for the interest of my own department, it is because I have never believed that classical study has any interest of any kind for or against the elective system, distinct from that of other departments of learning. I have steadily favored the change by which Greek and Latin have been made elective after the Freshman year, and I have done this in what I believed to be the best interests of classical scholarship as well as those of all other scholarship. As to the Freshman year, I have always thought that the elementary studies *once* required there belong to schools, and ought never to be taken into account in permanent plans of college study. The only escape from the increasing evils which surrounded us (under the old curriculum) was to be found in a plan by which no student should be required to take all studies, but every student should be allowed to give much more time and attention to certain branches which he elected than he could give to any of his studies before. It was clearly recognized that no partial or restricted schemes of elective study could help high scholarship.

"I regret as much as anybody the gaps which the elective system often leaves or allows careless students to leave in their education. I do not like to see young men go out from college stamped with the highest marks of honor, who have never read a line of the Iliad, who do not know what a syllogism is, or the difference between a planet and a fixed star. But when I look at these defects of our system and turn to the wonderful advance in scholarship which we owe to this same system, and especially when I think of how hopeless even our present scholarship seemed to us all twenty-five years ago, I cannot think we have made a mistake in securing this permanent gain. There is no necessity or inducement under our present system for anybody to exclude from his studies either Homer, Logic, or the elements of Astronomy. When we look on this place as a seat of learning, it is surely a nobler duty to open to everybody the highest instruction in every department than to prevent a few foolish persons from neglecting even important elementary branches." (*The Present and Future of Harvard College.*)

But as one ounce of fact is worth, in these uninspired days, many pounds of prophesying, let us see from statistics what has been the result at Harvard of making Latin and Greek elective. Five years ago, when substitutes for Latin and Greek were allowed in the entrance examinations for that University, this same cry was raised—that the study of Greek was doomed by such a radical step. On page 48 of the "*Report of the President of Harvard College*," for the year 1889–'90 (the last published), we read: "The provision of a substitute for elementary Greek or Latin *has had no effect on the latter;* the whole effect has been felt in Greek, which was omitted this year by about 8¼ per cent. of the candidates. This small percentage has been more than offset by the increase in the whole number of candidates, so that the absolute number of those presenting Greek has since 1888 materially increased. Down to 1886 Greek was prescribed for all candidates."

So that with Greek as an elective for entrance into Harvard, *over ninety per cent.* of the students still continue to prefer it and offer it.

Further comment seems to the Visitors unnecessary.

Your protest continues: "It is, doubtless, contended that the standard will not be lowered by the threatened change, because the professors will advance what are now their intermediate classes to the position which the senior classes occupy, and they in turn will be made more difficult. We apprehend that even supposing this to be true, it would be very undesirable, for there can be no possible complaint from any quarter that our senior classes are too easy. * * * Any material increase in the difficulty of our senior classes must place them in the list of postgraduate and special studies, and to that extent we close the door to the majority of students."

At the risk of being tedious, the Visitors must once more remind your committee that there is no longer in some of the most popular and most important Schools of the University any question of "Intermediate" and "Senior" classes. The work for the B. A. course is to be a collegiate work and is to have a distinctive character of its own, differing in methods, in scope, and in purpose from much of the work done in the old "Intermediate" classes.

Nor is the change a "threatened change." The change has been ordered and will be duly carried into effect.

It is certainly true that "there can be no possible complaint from any quarter that our senior classes are too easy." Such complaints, indeed, as have, from time to time, reached the ears of the Visitors have all been in a contrary direction—to-wit: that, in some classes, the requirements are unnecessarily hard.

It is pertinent to state here that the Visitors have noted in the printed protest, but more especially in a written supplemental paper, forwarded by the chairman of your committee, that you are mainly concerned as to how "easy" or how "hard" the new degrees are to be made, and, further, that you assume that the old degree is better because it is "*harder*." The Visitors venture to think that the whole point of view is erroneous. Because a course has been made "hard," it does not by any means follow that it has been made a sound, intelligent and beneficial course. But, judging from the past, we may safely trust the professors in the University to make both the B. A. and M. A. courses "hard" enough to satisfy the most rigid partisan of the old system.

When your committee says that "any material increase in the difficulty of our senior classes must place them in the rank of post-graduate and special studies and to that extent we close the door to the majority of students," you unconsciously make the very argument that long ago convinced the Visitors that the requirements of the old M. A. degree should be changed. While failing to make a man a real specialist in any one line of study, the training in some of the Schools, required under the curriculum, specialized too much for purposes of general culture even of an advanced kind, and it is almost unnecessary to again point out that a degree which, from 1885 to the present time, was taken by but *thirty* men, with an average attendance during these seven years of 200 academic students, effectually "closed the door to the majority of students." Restricted to the rigid old curriculum, if desirous of attaining any substantial distinction, but *one* in *forty-seven* secured "*the* degree."

That it should be claimed as the paramount glory of any University of our times, however "world-renowned," that, practically, her only reputable academic degree was one based upon a curriculum so rigid, that only *one* student out of every *forty-seven* could, or would, undergo the ordeal to secure this honor; that, ignoring the claims of the "newer learning" in science—nay, even the claims of our mother-tongue—for their proper place in any scheme of liberal education and academic award—she offered the remaining *forty-six*, no matter what their tastes or aptitudes, no other path, outside of the old "*artes liberales*" of the schoolmen, by which they might obtain from her some substantial mark of distinction; that this, above all, should be possible in the nineteenth century, in a university, that was, beyond all question, the first, among English-speaking people, to offer absolute freedom of election in liberal studies—surely, if the Visitors may be allowed for once to borrow the spirit of prophecy, all this is something that intelligent people in the twentieth century will find hard to believe.

It is the crying evil of this state of things, so fraught with manifest injury to the best interests of the University, that the Visitors are now striving to remedy.

"But this result," you continue, "we do not dread so much as that other and we fear more probable conse-

quence, to-wit: that in the effort to popularize and populate their classes, the professors will bend from that high
and rigid standard which has made the University world-
renowned. A student who has the choice of many departments for his degree will inevitably like those which can
be attained with least difficulty; a large falling off will
follow in those Schools which are intrinsically more difficult, though, for that reason, perhaps more useful, and
the professor must stand by and see his School decimated,
or must make it more popular at the expense of the requisite labor and usefulness. It is not hard to conceive which
course he will adopt."

It may "not" be "hard" for some of you "to conceive
what course he will adopt," but it is "hard" for the Visitors to "conceive" how others of the gentlemen who signed
this protest could ever have sanctioned these words, which
directly impugn the honesty, sincerity and devotion of
every academic professor in this University.

If there is one thing, beyond all others, that distin-
guishes the true scholar from the charlatan, it is his sin-
gle-minded loyalty to the high ideals of his profession, and
his absolute devotion to the work that he has elected as
his life-work.

To say of any professor that he is a man who is likely
to seek to "popularize" his class by pandering to the ig-
noble demands of idle students ambitious of academic
honors, is to say that he is a demagogue of the most con-
temptible type—a time-serving apostle of cheap electro-
plate culture.

The Visitors willingly allow that your committee, as a
whole, cannot be conscious of the gravity of such language,
and that this utterly gratuitous bit of prophecy would
never have been sanctioned by some, at least, of the signers of the protest, had they paused to consider what such
language implied.

The Visitors are the more confident of this charitable construction, because some of these gentlemen have assured them personally that they signed the protest without seriously considering it, "merely to oblige others."

Happily, the imputation of this paragraph is too fully refuted by the conduct of the professors in the past, to need any serious consideration at the hands of the Visitors.

If ever in the history of the University there was a time when the temptation to "popularize" all classes was most insidious, it was in the years immediately succeeding the war, when the fortunes of this institution were in desperate condition. But in no "School," either within or without the curriculum required for the old degree, did a single professor seek to "populate" his School by a depreciated standard.

If any mistake was made, it seems to the Visitors that it was rather in the direction of advancing the standard beyond what could be reasonably expected of young men, who, for four years, had been denied the advantages of systematic training under competent teachers.

If your further prophecy be true, that "a student who has the choice of many departments for his degree will inevitably take those which can be attained with least difficulty," then Thomas Jefferson made a tremendous blunder in discarding the old curriculum, and was only a short-sighted enthusiast in believing that young men, disdaining to consider how "hard" or how "easy" any subject of study might be, would pursue the "best in learning for true learning's sake."

The Visitors do not deem it necessary to enter upon any consideration of the supplemental MS. paper inclosed with the printed protest, as that paper is chiefly devoted to a discussion of points which do not seem to them to have any essential connection with the question at issue. It deals mainly with the "reputation" of the *ante-bellum* and *post-bellum* M. A. degrees, and institutes afresh many comparisons as to how "hard" and how "easy" the old and the new M. A. degrees are respectively.

An article on the new degrees, contributed to the *University Magazine* for November, 1891, by the "Chairman of the M. A. Committee," has also been sent to the Board as part of your argument. The Board must presume that this article was forwarded without the sanction of the committee, as its general tone is certainly not such as would be likely to win a considerate hearing from those who do not absolutely share the dogmatic opinions of the writer.

The Visitors have not, of course, directly or indirectly, taken any part in the discussions touching the new degrees that have appeared in the public press, nor do they propose to do so.

They have given this lengthy explanation of the reasons impelling them to make the changes against which you protest, not merely as a matter of courtesy, but in the belief that many of your committee will see the imperative necessity of the steps taken, now that the whole matter has been fully and fairly presented to them.

But with this explanation, which is offered in a spirit of perfect frankness and kindness, the discussion, so far as the Visitors are concerned, ends.

To sum up:

It has seemed to the Visitors (and they have so ordered) that the three degrees in the Academic Department of the University should have the following aim and scope:

I.—B. A.—A degree of general culture designed for the great body of students, in which little restriction shall be placed upon the student in regard to election of studies beyond the fact that no one of the five great departments of human learning—An-

cient Languages, Modern Languages, Mathematical Sciences, Natural and Physical Sciences, Historical and Philosophical Sciences—may be altogether neglected. The requirements are graduation in eight (8) B. A. Courses. Standard ¾.

II.—M. A.—A degree for advanced University work, open
to such students as shall have first attained the
B. A. degree, either in this University, or at some
other chartered institution of learning, provided,
in the latter case, that the Faculty shall deem such
degree the full equivalent of the B. A. degree granted here; and further provided, that the candidate
shall, *in all cases*, be a graduate in the B. A. courses
in this University of such Schools as he elects for
his advanced work. The degree is designed for
those who propose to make teaching a profession,
and also for such students as, through love of
learning, desire to pursue their studies beyond the
B. A. courses. The requirements are graduation
in four (4) University "Schools," approved by the
Faculty. Standard ¾.

III.—PH. D.—A degree for specialists, open to such students
as shall have first attained the degree of B. A. or
M. A. in this University, or at some other chartered institution of learning, provided, in this latter case, that the Faculty shall deem such degree
the full equivalent of the B. A. degree granted here.
This degree demands very high attainments, in
some special lines of study, and these attainments
must be proved, (1) by a thesis, showing an original treatment of some fitting subject or giving
satisfactory evidence of the power of *independent*
investigation; and (2) by the candidate's passing

successfully rigid examinations on some two subjects elected by the student for his graduate work.

These two subjects are to be approved by the Faculty. No candidate is to be admitted to examination until his thesis has also been approved. On successfully passing his examination, the candidate may print his thesis, along with the certificate of approval granted by the examiners.

The Visitors are fully aware of the responsibility they have assumed in ordering these changes, nor do they seek in any way to shirk this responsibility.

They believe that these changes should long ago have been made, and they have abundant reason to believe that already the weight of intelligent opinion in the State heartily supports them in the step they have taken.

But, in any event, they are resolved to do their duty to the University and to the best interests of the higher education throughout the South, as they see it, and are entirely confident that time will vindicate the wisdom of their action. They may add that they will always be glad to receive from any intelligent source such suggestions touching modifications in the degree courses as time and experience will, no doubt, dictate.

We are, gentlemen, with high respect,

Your obedient servants,

W. C. N. RANDOLPH, Rector,
CAMM PATTESON,
THOMAS S. MARTIN,
MARSHALL McCORMICK,
R. L. PARRISH,
R. W. MARTIN,
R. G. H. KEAN,
BASIL B. GORDON,
W. GORDON McCABE.

www.ingramcontent.com/pod-product-compliance
Lightning Source LLC
Chambersburg PA
CBHW022031080426

42733CB00007B/804